INSIDE LAW ENFORCEMENT

INSIDE LAW ENFORCE
ENFORCEMENT
IN
INSIDE LAW ENFORCE

INSIDE ICE

U.S. IMMIGRATION & CUSTOMS ENFORCEMENT

Mythili Sampathkumar

Enslow Publishing
101 W. 23rd Street
Suite 240
New York, NY 10011
USA

enslow.com

Published in 2020 by Enslow Publishing, LLC
101 W. 23rd Street, Suite 240, New York, NY 10011

Library of Congress Cataloging-in-Publication Data

Names: Sampathkumar, Mythili, author.
Title: Inside ICE / Mythili Sampathkumar.
Description: New York : Enslow Publishing, 2020. | Series: Inside law enforcement | Includes bibliographical references and index. | Audience: Grade 5 to 8.
Identifiers: LCCN 2018058099| ISBN 9781978507371 (library bound) | ISBN 9781978508491 (pbk.)
Subjects: LCSH: U.S. Immigration and Customs Enforcement—Juvenile literature. | Illegal aliens—Government policy—United States. | United States—Emigration and immigration—Government policy—Juvenile literature.
Classification: LCC JV6483 .S26 2020 | DDC 363.25/9370973—dc23
LC record available at https://lccn.loc.gov/2018058099

Printed in the United States of America

To Our Readers: We have done our best to make sure all website addresses in this book were active and appropriate when we went to press. However, the author and the publisher have no control over and assume no liability for the material available on those websites or on any websites they may link to. Any comments or suggestions can be sent by email to customerservice@enslow.com.

Photo Credits: Cover, pp. 1, 14, 23 John Moore/Getty Images; pp. 5, 21 The Washington Post/Getty Images; p. 7 Spencer Platt/Getty Images; p. 8 Al Rai Al Aam/Feature Story News/Getty Images; p. 13 Mark Ralston/AFP/Getty Images; p. 17 Alex Milan Tracy/Sipa USA/Newscom; p. 24 Nuangthong/Shutterstock.com; pp. 27, 30 © AP Images; p. 28 Robyn Beck/AFP/Getty Images; p. 34 Chip Somodevilla/Getty Images; p. 36 Drew Angerer/Getty Images; p. 38 Wichita Eagle/Tribune News Service/Getty Images.

CONTENTS

INTRODUCTION

The Immigration and Customs Enforcement (ICE) agency was formed in 2003 by President George W. Bush as part of the effort to combine and consolidate several border protection, immigration, and port security services into one agency. It was formed by combining several functions from the previous Immigration and Naturalization Service (INS) and US Customs Service agencies under one roof. As a result, it is the second largest agency under its parent, the Department of Homeland Security (DHS).

ICE has been given a fairly broad range of powers—from enforcing US immigration laws and customs rules to investigating terrorist activity. Those main tasks are reflected in the two overarching divisions of the federal agency, which are Homeland Security Investigations (HSI) and Enforcement and Removal Operations (ERO). However, the agency often gets confused with US Border Patrol, which is actually run through ICE's sister agency under the DHS, US Customs and Border Protection (CBP). The two agencies perform separate functions, and this book will describe in more detail ICE's tasks, such as immigration and naturalization services, border protection, port security, customs and duties management, and counterterrorism operations.

ICE is the second largest contributor to the Joint Terrorism Task Force, a partnership of several federal, state, and local law enforcement agencies set up to help coordinate and combine efforts to fight terrorism. The agency employs approximately twenty thousand people in four hundred different offices in America and forty-six other countries. Its headquarters are in Washington, DC. It has a budget of $7.6 billion[1].

Although ICE has only been around since 2003, it has been no stranger to political debates and controversies. Most notably, critics have called for the abolishment of the agency over issues like family separation in the summer of 2018, when the agency was tasked

ICE has come under fire in recent years for its treatment of immigrants and refugees, leading to protests of its actions and the agency as a whole.

with separating children from parents and guardians as they entered the country illegally at the US-Mexico border.

The acting director in 2018 was Ronald Vitiello, who was appointed to the position by President Donald Trump on June 30, 2018. He previously served as the acting deputy commissioner of the CBP and chief of the US Border Patrol. Vitiello reported to the secretary of DHS, Kirstjen Nielsen.

Throughout this book, you'll learn about the short but storied history of this unique law enforcement agency, how and why ICE officers do their work, and how people across the country and around the world have responded to the agency's actions.

CHAPTER 1

THE HISTORY OF ICE

On September 11, 2001, four passenger flights traveling from the northeast United States to California were hijacked by nineteen individuals affiliated with the terrorist group al-Qaeda. The terrorists purposely crashed two planes into the Twin Towers of the World Trade Center in New York City, and one plane crashed into the Department of Defense headquarters at the Pentagon near Washington, DC. The fourth plane landed in a field in Shanksville, Pennsylvania, after passengers on board fought the hijackers for control of the plane.

The terrorist attacks of September 11, 2001, resulted in nearly three thousand people dying and more than six thousand injured. It also made the country take a harder look at immigration because the terrorists involved had entered, lived, and gone to flight school in the United States ahead of the tragic events.

The terrorist attacks on the World Trade Center in New York City on September 11, 2001, led to the creation of ICE.

America's New Security Measures

Congress passed—and President George W. Bush signed into law—the Homeland Security Act[1] in November 2002, dissolving the former Immigration and Naturalization Service, the US Customs Service, and the Federal Protective Service and replacing them with several new agencies under the umbrella of the Department of Homeland Security, which was tasked with protecting the country from another potential act of terrorism.

The DHS secretary became a cabinet-level position in the Bush administration and oversees twenty-four sub-agencies, including the Coast Guard and Secret Service. It was the single largest government

THE AFTERMATH OF 9/11

The 9/11 terrorist attacks killed nearly three thousand people from the United States and ninety other countries, injured more than six thousand, and prompted the country and the administration of President George W. Bush to take a hard look at the immigration policies that allowed the terrorists to enter, live in, and go to flight school in America. The attacks also led to the US war in Afghanistan, where it was thought the mastermind of the attacks, Osama bin Laden, had been hiding.

Osama bin Laden was behind the 9/11 attacks on America, which led to the creation of ICE.

Under President Barack Obama, bin Laden was killed in 2011 in Pakistan, but the US war in Afghanistan continued against various terrorist groups that reside in the country.

reorganization since the country created the Department of Defense on September 18, 1947, in the wake of World War II[2].

One of the new agencies created under the Homeland Security Act was the Bureau of Border Security, which was renamed Immigration and Customs Enforcement (ICE) and began operating in March 2003. INS functions were thus split between ICE, the new US Citizenship and Immigration Services (USCIS), and the Transportation Security Administration (TSA), also known as airport security. There was also a sister agency created under DHS, US Customs and Border Protection (CBP). The shift and creation of agencies was a chaotic but fairly quick move, and it changed forever how America enforced immigration laws and how citizens traveled and dealt with the threat of terrorism.

A Bigger Threat Than Terrorism

ICE was formed into four main divisions: Homeland Security Investigations (HSI), Enforcement and Removal Operations (ERO), the Office of the Principal Legal Advisor (OPLA), and Management and Administration, which supports the other three. The agency began training special agents in its first year.

Michael Garcia was confirmed by the Senate in November 2003 and served as the first assistant secretary of the new agency. ICE had 15,000 employees and a budget of $4 billion. Its 2018 budget hovered around $7.6 billion, and there were approximately 20,000 employees. The number of employees is in part determined by the budget, which must be approved by Congress every year.

While the agency was founded to stop terrorism after the September 11 attacks, much of what ICE does has nothing to do with terrorists. The agency has worked to protect America's borders from not only terrorists like those in al-Qaeda who were responsible for 9/11, but also dangerous gangs from South and Central America.

Terrorism was the big concern for ICE during the agency's early years, but as the threat of terror attacks on American soil began to lessen following the death of Osama bin Laden, new threats began to take prominence. Gangs like MS13 started to grow in the US, so it became part of ICE's job to stop new members from Central American countries like El Salvador, Honduras, and Guatemala from crossing the southern US border.

Unfortunately for the agency, the new focus on the US-Mexico border led to many controversies and claims that the agency and the agents working for it were racist against Latinx people. In 2017 and 2018, the law enforcement agency came under attack for its border control practices, and protests were staged across the country calling for an end to these security measures—and to ICE itself.

Using Technology to Keep America Safe

ICE's security measures are not only about border patrol and keeping the bad guys out of the country. The agency also uses technology to monitor potential threats within the country. Through its Electronic Monitoring Program, it's able to keep track of people it believes could be threats but who it has no reason to bar from entry to the US or deport.

But it's not just about people. ICE also manages an inter-agency project, the Intellectual Property Rights Coordination Center, that works to keep harmful products from entering the United States. Through its work on intellectual property protections, ICE makes sure that dangerous counterfeit products are prevented from entering the country and harming American citizens. It also works with other intelligence and law enforcement agencies to make sure that the intellectual property of

Americans is protected. That means making sure that counterfeiters who wrongly replicate American products are punished, and that American businesses do not have their copyrights, trademarks, or patents violated by foreign companies. While this may seem different from ICE's other security activities, protecting Americans from any foreign threat on American soil is the agency's prime agenda, and that includes protecting American citizens from bad actors in the foreign business sector.

CHAPTER 2

WHAT DOES ICE DO?

According to the agency's website, "ICE's primary mission is to promote homeland security and public safety through the criminal and civil enforcement of federal laws governing border control, customs, trade, and immigration."[1] The three main divisions of ICE that perform these duties are Homeland Security Investigations (HSI), Enforcement and Removal Operations (ERO), and the Office of the Principal Legal Advisor (OPLA).

The main functions carried out by the agency can be roughly categorized as immigration and naturalization services, border protection, port security, customs and duties management, and counterterrorism operations. Much of what the divisions of ICE do is influenced by who the president is at the time, and this chapter will include notes on how policies have changed or stayed the same through the administrations of Presidents George W. Bush, Barack Obama, and Donald Trump.

ICE, along with US Border Patrol, is responsible for policing the 2,000-mile-long border between the US and Mexico, some of which is lined with a border wall.

Investigative Work

With 6,500 special agents and 8,300 total employees, the HSI is the largest division of DHS and the second largest investigative division in the entire US government. These agents are tasked with looking into any matters that may be risks to the national security of the country, which means there is a wide variety of casework. ICE agents have handled cases and pursued criminals involved in drug trafficking, human trafficking, weapons smuggling, and counterfeit immigration documents. Investigators also handle financial crimes, fraud, art or cultural property theft, counterfeit pharmaceutical drugs, and cyber crimes,

One of ICE's roles is to make sure that immigrants who are to be deported actually comply and leave the country as ordered, as these Guatemalan deportees did.

since any of these could be tied to financing terrorist operations or attacking the country.

Enforcement and Removal Operations

What ICE is best known for are its deportation operations, which the agency refers to as "removal" operations. The job of Enforcement and Removal Operations (ERO) is to detain and deport people who enter the United States illegally or remain in the country without legal paperwork.

ICE calls immigrants eligible for deportation "removable aliens" and has seven different categories people may fall under:

1. Immigrants who have been convicted of any type of criminal offense.
2. Those charged with a criminal offense that has not been resolved in the court system or other legal proceeding.
3. Any immigrant, documented or not, who has committed acts that "constitute a chargeable criminal offense."
4. People who have "engaged in fraud or willful misrepresentation in connection with any official matter before a governmental agency," meaning an immigrant who lied to the government on paperwork or during questioning to gain legal entry into the United States.
5. Immigrants determined to have abused a public benefits program like welfare, social security, or Medicaid/Medicare health care programs.
6. Any immigrant who received an order for deportation but did not comply with the requirement.
7. Any person whom an ICE agent or immigration officer determines is a risk to public safety or national security.

The ERO had about 7,900 employees and a $3.8 billion budget in 2017. Under President Barack Obama, the ERO focused on removing immigrants who had committed serious crimes while in the country without proper documents. That changed under President Donald Trump, who broadened that policy to include any people in the country without the proper legal paperwork.[2]

For an idea of the size of this part of ICE's operations, in the 2017 fiscal year, which ended on September 30, the agency deported, or removed, approximately 226,000 people from the United States.[3] That was down 6 percent from 2016 deportations. In fact, there were fewer deportations in 2017 than at any time during the Obama administration, according to previous DHS data.

However, ICE also arrests immigrants who have been suspected of entering or remaining in the country illegally. In the 2017 fiscal year, ICE arrested 111,000 people, which was a 42 percent increase from the previous year.

One of the ERO's functions is prevention of illegal immigration, so people are deterred from attempting to enter the country improperly in the future. In the 2017 fiscal year, 216,000 people tried to enter the United States through various ports and borders. That is a decrease of 23.7 percent from 2016.[4]

A majority of the immigrants in detention or deported from the United States came here from Central American countries, including Honduras, Guatemala, and El Salvador. When these immigrants are deported or removed, they often are tried in special immigration courts. There is an entire branch of law devoted to issues of immigration, and ICE works with lawyers whose job it is to interpret immigration law for them and assist the immigrants in their efforts to remain in the United States.

How to Become an ICE Agent

There are several career paths you can take if you want to work for ICE: deportation or removal officer, detention officer, criminal investigator, technical enforcement investigator, and administrative or management roles.

With four hundred offices spread across all fifty states and forty-seven countries around the world, there is a wealth of options. Even as the Trump administration attempts to trim the federal budget, fighting terrorism and illegal immigration, as well as protecting US borders, remain high priorities with relatively steady funding.[5]

One of the highest-profile roles in the agency is that of ICE special agent, and DHS has minimum requirements that must be met.

ICE agents don't work only along the US-Mexico border, but also in satellite offices around the country and along the US-Canada border.

ICE special agents must be at least twenty-one years old and have a bachelor's degree from an accredited university with a 3.5 grade point average (GPA) in courses related to their major and at least a 3.0 GPA in other subjects. Superior applicants are encouraged to have at least a

SPECIAL RESPONSE TEAMS

The Special Response Team (SRT) under the HSI is essentially the agency's special weapons and tactics (SWAT) team. SRT members come from the highly trained pool of ICE agents, and out of 6,500 special agents, approximately 250 have passed the rigorous testing to become SRT members. The teams carry out very high-risk arrest and search warrants, perform operations in rural areas, protect certain important figures, provide sniper coverage, and provide general security. SRTs are headquartered in each of the seventeen ICE field offices, including in border areas like El Paso, Texas, and major international hubs like New York and Washington, DC.

year of graduate-level coursework under their belts as well, particularly for investigative roles, as a written test is required.

Medical exams, drug tests, and a background investigation are also required to work for ICE.

The agency says it is looking for law enforcement officers with "integrity and courage."[6] Being in excellent physical shape, having an ability to handle stressful environments, and demonstrating critical thinking skills are all key qualities ICE looks for in prospective agents. Military veterans are given certain age and education requirement waivers depending on the length and type of service.

Most important to the agency, however, is that all employees be committed to protecting the United States from cross-border criminal activity, including terrorism and illegal immigration.

If hired to become an Enforcement and Removal Operations officer, individuals will start their job training with several weeks of lessons to learn Spanish, given the majority of people detained or deported from the United States are, in 2018, from Spanish-speaking countries. They will also be required to complete the rigorous sixteen-week Basic Immigration Enforcement Training Program at the Federal Law Enforcement Training Center, where agents from all federal law enforcement agencies go to train.

There are no less than seven tests and a physical assessment during the training program, all of which a prospective agent must pass with at least a 70 percent grade.[7] The whole process can take up to two hundred days.

CHAPTER 3

ICE AND IMMIGRATION LAW

ICE's most recognizable function is deporting individuals who are in the United States without proper documentation. Sometimes, these cases end up becoming high profile as the media, politicians, and the public weigh in. In more than one case, a person who had been living in the country for decades was deported to a place they barely knew.

While the organizational structure of the Department of Homeland Security may be a bit confusing, all the divisions have the same goal of enforcing US immigration law as it changes, regardless of who is in Congress or the White House. While the debate among politicians rages on as to whether and how to change immigration laws, ICE continues its work through removals, investigation, and intelligence gathering.

Headquartered in Washington, DC, ICE not only acts as an enforcement agency with officers patrolling the border, it also does electronic monitoring and verification of immigrant workers.

One of the main ways ICE enforces immigration law is by monitoring American workplaces and exposing the employment of undocumented immigrants.[1] Through the ICE Mutual Agreement Between Government and Employers (IMAGE) program, companies are certified through training programs. Companies that want protection from large workplace raids—in which undocumented immigrants are rounded up and determined to be removable or not—must enroll in DHS's E-Verify system. E-Verify is an electronic system that helps employers determine if a person is eligible for legal employment in the United States.

ICE also conducts periodic audits of the Employee Eligibility Verification Form, or Form I-9, which immigrant employees must submit to US employers when they begin working. Companies not in compliance have been forced to pay fines and lay off thousands of immigrant workers in the past.

One high-profile element of immigration law that ICE deals with is the 287(g) program. This program allows the DHS secretary to enter into cooperation agreements with state and local law enforcement agencies in order to make communication and information sharing between ICE and these parties more efficient and effective. Some members of local law enforcement welcomed the law, but others came out against it.

Under the direction of ICE agents, local police officers are trained to identify and even detain individuals who may have entered or remain in the United States illegally. Critics of the program have said that it increases racial profiling—or targeting a person based on their race or ethnicity because of stereotypes of that person's race or group, rather than being suspicious of the individual. It is just one of the controversial issues with ICE.

Intra-Agency Cooperation

In theory, the sister agencies of ICE and CBP work in tandem to enforce the country's immigration laws. US Customs and Border Protection is supposed to work at the borders, while ICE has been tasked with focusing on the rest of the country. The lines can get blurred, depending on the case, but each agency operates separately yet cooperatively under the DHS umbrella.

There are 325 ports of entry into the United States, and CBP has been given the authority to detain, question, and investigate anyone coming into the country through any one of these entry points.[2]

The US Border Patrol sits within Customs and Border Protection, and its agents are charged with doing the actual patrolling of the US border areas, where its main mission is "the detection and apprehension of illegal aliens and smugglers of aliens at or near the land border."[3]

The distinction is that Border Patrol has the authorization to arrest, detain, and investigate "aliens" within 99 miles (160 kilometers) of US land and coastal borders. This area actually covers nearly two-thirds of the population given the location of most major American cities.

Border Patrol also helps with anti-smuggling operations, controls traffic checkpoints along highways, and conducts checks of vehicles traveling on highways leading to border areas.

ICE can't do the job alone, so it works closely with Customs and Border Protection, local law enforcement, and other federal agencies in order to best protect the country.

Deportation

Only ICE has the authority to deport "removable aliens," however, and its lawyers are able to represent the agency and the US government as a whole in legal proceedings.

In January 2018, Amer Adi Othman[4] of Youngstown, Ohio, was deported back to Jordan despite living in the United States for nearly forty years, starting a family, and building a business here. ICE had determined that Othman had no legal right to stay in the country because his first wife said their marriage was not legitimate. She later took back what she said and wrote a statement about it.

In another case, a Nazi labor camp guard named Jakiw Palij[5] was deported back to Germany in August 2018 after he had been living in New York since 1949. Palij had lied about his ties to the Nazis during

ICE doesn't only work to remove illegal immigrants. It also works closely with the agencies that are responsible for helping legal immigrants stay in the country and potentially become citizens.

WWII, when he came to the United States and even became a citizen in 1957. Some thirty years later, authorities found his name in old records and had been attempting to deport him ever since.

Joel Colindres[6] fled violence in Guatemala in 2004. After working in the United States, he married his girlfriend Samantha, a US citizen, and had two children. What Colindres did not realize was that he had missed an important hearing with immigration authorities, which had resulted in a deportation order. After years spent filing legal paperwork and checking in with authorities, he was forced to go back to Guatemala in February 2018.

Coming to America to Stay

A third organization also handles immigration matters under the DHS: US Citizenship and Immigration Services (USCIS). This agency is tasked with processing and approving applications for visas, resident alien status or "green cards," and citizenship. USCIS, unlike its co-agencies, is not a law enforcement body but does work in conjunction with the other two as needed.

When someone comes to America legally, they must work with USCIS to obtain the proper paperwork in order to be permitted entrance. If a person wants to come to America for only a short time, for a job or for school, they must apply for a visa that allows them to stay in the country for a period of several months or years. However, if a person wants to stay in the US longer, they have to apply for resident alien status, or a green card, and eventually citizenship. While USCIS works with people to make sure they have all the proper paperwork and can stay as long as they need to, ICE works to make sure that anyone who stays longer than they're allowed either returns to their home country or is able to get new paperwork from USCIS in order to legally extend their stay.

CHAPTER 4

CONTROVERSIAL DECISIONS

Like any federal agency, particularly a law enforcement agency, ICE has encountered its share of controversial issues. From its beginning, some Americans worried about the backlash against Muslim, Sikh, and other non-white immigrants in the wake of the September 11 attacks. The establishment of ICE, in their minds, solidified that fear.

Others feel the United States should have more open borders to allow those fleeing gang and drug-related violence and rampant poverty in Central America a chance at a better life in the United States and a pathway to becoming citizens.

ICE operates several detention centers, or jails, for people the agency has caught attempting to enter the United States without proper legal documents or those who have overstayed their visas. There are nearly 1,500[3] detention facilities in the United States, housing approximately 39,000 adults on any given day in 2018. That count includes county jails,

Bureau of Prisons facilities, Office of Refugee Resettlement centers, hospitals, and hotels used by ICE.

Death in Detention

Some of the more high-profile controversies involving ICE include deaths in ICE detention centers.[1]

The data on the number and nature of deaths is not easily obtained because government agencies like the Department of Homeland Secu-

When ICE arrests someone, the person is sent to a special ICE detention center, where they wait to either be allowed to stay or get deported back to the country they arrived from.

While some detention centers, like the one above, are modern and comparable to American jails, others are very sparse, leading to protests against ICE for what some say is inhumane treatment of detainees.

rity often cite protection of national security as a reason not to make that information public. However, in 2010, the *New York Times* and the American Civil Liberties Union (ACLU) filed a Freedom of Information Act request and determined that at least 107 people had died[2] in ICE detention facilities between 2003, when the agency was established, and 2007.

A look at the circumstances surrounding the deaths appeared to show the cause of death for those ICE detainees was related to a lack of proper medical care despite repeated requests for aid.

A 2018 report from Human Rights Watch[4], which included analysis by several independent medical experts, showed the same after examining the cases of fifteen detainee deaths between December 2015 and April 2017.

According to the report, "Eight of the 15 public death reviews show that inadequate medical care contributed or led to the person's death. The physicians conducting the analysis also found evidence of substandard medical practices in all but one of the remaining reviews."

In 2017 alone, twelve detainees had died in ICE facilities—more than in any year except 2009. From March 2010 to April 2017, there were seventy-four total deaths. At the time the report was published, ICE had released information about fifty-two of the cases.

Family Separation

Detainee deaths are a controversial topic, but the Trump administration's zero-tolerance policy sparked global outrage when it was first enacted in May 2018. Trump's hard line against illegal immigration meant that

DETAINED

The facility with the largest number of detained immigrants in 2017 was the Stewart Detention Center, a private prison in Lumpkin, Georgia, which held 1,917 people at the time. The majority of ICE's detention centers are located along the US-Mexico border in Texas and California. Florida, Colorado, and New York also have large numbers of facilities. Sometimes, the facilities include large chain hotels or empty warehouse-style buildings, like the facility located next to the IKEA store in Brooklyn, New York. Others look more like prisons or makeshift tent cities

Under President Trump, a record number of children were separated from their parents at the US–Mexico border and sent to detention centers alone.

the Justice Department would treat all people attempting to cross the border without authorization as criminals and would attempt to prosecute them. When families attempted to cross the border illegally, this policy meant that parents were taken into custody—and because the detention centers are supposed to act as jails, this meant that they were separated from their children, who were turned over to ICE custody as "unaccompanied minors."

More than two thousand children had been taken from parents and guardians as they illegally crossed into the United States at the Mexico border in the weeks the policy, instituted by Attorney General Jeff Sessions, was active.

The children rounded up during this period were kept in various detention facilities and were sometimes taken from siblings because of age restrictions in the facilities. The parents and guardians were charged with a crime, even those seeking asylum in the United States, and children were unable to enter the US criminal justice system. Trump's executive order declared that "family unity" will be maintained "where appropriate and consistent with law and available resources."

The Trump administration repeatedly said it was "the law" to separate families for reasons of safety and to combat human trafficking at the border. However, there is no US immigration law or court precedent that compels the federal government to separate families. The policy laid out in May 2018 by Sessions essentially made seeking asylum—which, according to US law, requires entry into the country first—a crime. Thus, when families seeking asylum crossed the border, the parents were arrested while the children were separated and sent to their own detention centers.

There were weeks of angry protests and public comments from members of Congress, governors, mayors, former government officials, world leaders, and even former First Ladies—both Democrats and Republicans. Several media reports with audio and video of children crying and screaming out for their family members were published, prompting the president to sign an executive order[5] on June 20, 2018, rescinding the policy.

A court order ensured the federal government would have to reunite families—whether in ICE detention facilities, their home countries, or with relatives legally in the country—by a certain deadline. However, medical professionals said the trauma of being away from their families for even several weeks could already have long-lasting effects on the children.[6]

CHAPTER 5

THE FUTURE OF ICE

The fate of ICE and other DHS agencies depends largely on Congress and the president, and because control of the executive and legislative branches of government changes every four years, the future of ICE is uncertain.

With more immigrants coming to the United States every year and techniques to fight terrorism changing every day, there may come a time when the agency has outlived its usefulness. As the section in this book on controversies proved, there are many people who believe that the agency has already become obsolete and should be abolished.

The process to abolish the organization would require Congress to pass new legislation, but more than that, it would require a change in what American voters want.

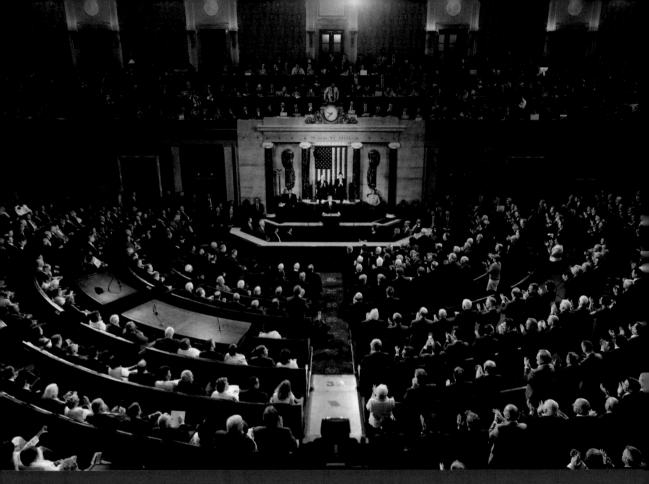

ICE's future will be determined by Congress. The US House and Senate have the power to fund ICE or defund and abolish the controversial agency.

Abolish ICE?

In the wake of the controversy over family separations, thousands of Americans joined a political movement to eliminate the agency altogether.[1] One of the arguments made for abolishing ICE is that the agency is very young and therefore we know that we can get along fine without it. Those in favor of shutting down ICE say that other, more established law enforcement agencies can absorb the investigative, intelligence, and counterterrorism work being done by ICE and do it better.

Though it may appear the movement is spearheaded by Democrats, or at least those who do not identify as Republicans, several immigrants' rights advocates were frustrated with President Barack Obama's expansion of the agency and record number of deportations during his two terms in office and began arguing for an end to ICE while it was controlled by the Obama administration. However, the movement gained popularity in the wake of President Trump's inauguration and his proposal to build a nearly 2,000-mile (3,218-km) wall along the US-Mexico border to stem illegal immigration.

The movement soon found a home on social media, where it was spread with the #AbolishICE hashtag, which was first used by Sean McElwee, a cofounder of the think tank Data for Progress. Politicians running for office in 2018 took up the call to abolish ICE, using their position on the agency as a way of signaling their values to voters. One of the most outspoken candidates in the #AbolishICE movement during

ICE AND THE PRIVATE SECTOR

As with any government agency, ICE holds contracts with private companies[2] and even universities to fill functions it feels the government can't do or, at least, can't do for the same cost to the American taxpayer. For instance, ICE has paid Microsoft almost $20 million to provide the agency with email, calendar, messaging, and document management services[3], while Dell has been contracted to provide the agency with computers and software. Northeastern University helps with analyzing data. Johns Hopkins University and the Vermont State Colleges system have agreed to provide education and training services to agency employees. Other private-sector business partners for ICE include the accounting firms Ernst & Young and Deloitte, copier and printer companies like Xerox and Canon, internet service and cable companies Time Warner and Comcast, and delivery services like Amazon and UPS. All of these contracts are reviewed periodically and subject to government regulations.

the 2018 midterms was Alexandria Ocasio-Cortez, who was elected as a congresswoman from New York.

Even ICE agents have called for splitting the agency. Nineteen agents and ICE leaders wrote an open letter to DHS secretary Kirstjen Nielsen asking her to have the agency focus on Homeland Security Investigations, the crime-fighting operations of ICE, instead of the deportations conducted by the Enforcement and Removal Operations arm. The group wrote that several ICE agents "have been perceived as targeting undocumented aliens, instead of the transnational criminal

Protests against ICE grew throughout 2018, as the agency faced a multitude of scandals. Whether the agency will survive, however, has yet to be determined.

organizations that facilitate cross border crimes impacting our communities and national security,"[4] and so these agents wanted the two arms of the agency split into independent entities. However, others have asked an important question: If ICE were abolished, what would replace it?

Any move to change or eliminate the agency would not happen overnight, and neither would reallocating the billions of dollars in its budget. Some experts and scholars have argued that the agency's functions, outlined earlier in this book, could be carried out by other law enforcement agencies, and that Customs and Border Patrol could be better regulated if the task of monitoring the vast US border were left to other agencies and their procedures.

Others have said ICE provides a crucial service in protecting America from another terrorist attack and from being so open that even those with criminal records are able to enter freely with little fear of consequence. They fear a system—and a border—that is as open as that in place in many European countries, some of which take in millions of migrants and refugees each year.

The Schengen Area is a collection of twenty-six countries on the European continent that have gotten rid of individual passports and border control functions. It allows for relatively free travel and police cooperation through a shared information database, among other elements.

One point is clear: The recent controversies surrounding ICE have made Americans think about and discuss the agency in a way that people have not done since its inception in 2003. Where that national conversation leads is up to the citizens, who will have to decide what kind of country they want the United States to be for immigrants and travelers from around the world.

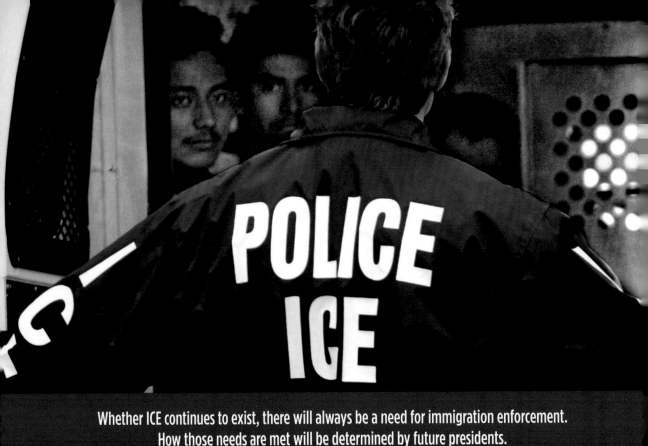

Whether ICE continues to exist, there will always be a need for immigration enforcement. How those needs are met will be determined by future presidents.

What Does the Future Hold?

Whether ICE is ever abolished will depend on who runs the country and how the political climate changes over the years. When ICE was first established in the aftermath of the September 11, 2001, terrorist attacks, very few people doubted the importance of the agency. The threat to America and its citizens was so great, and the fear people felt so strong, that it was hard for people to imagine the agency doing anything but helping to ease those fears by securing the country's borders. However, as times changed and threats to American security changed, people's feelings about ICE also changed.

ICE's future is going to be determined not by its actual work, but by the value people see in protecting America's borders. When the threat was terrorism, it was very easy for the government to rally support for the agency and get people on both ends of the political spectrum to agree that the government should do as much as possible to keep certain people out of the country. With terrorism no longer a major threat to Americans, it has become harder for people to justify ICE's actions and existence.

One thing is certain, however: Immigration enforcement and border protection will be an important topic in political conversations for years to come, and ICE, whether it remains, changes, or is abolished, will be a part of those conversations.

CHAPTER NOTES

Introduction

1. "In 2017, the Government Spent $3.98 Trillion," USASpending.gov, https://www.usaspending.gov/#/.

Chapter 1: The History of ICE

1. "Immigration and Customs Enforcement: Who We Are," ICE.gov, https://www.ice.gov.

2. "Immigration and Customs Enforcement: History of ICE," ICE.gov, https://www.ice.gov.

Chapter 2: What Does ICE Do?

1. "U.S. Immigration and Customs Enforcement: What We Do" ICE. gov, https://www.ice.gov.

2. Elliot Young, "The Hard Truths About Obama's Deportation Priorities," Huffington Post, February 27, 2017, https://www.huffingtonpost.com/entry/hard-truths-about-obamas-deportation-priorities_us_58b-3c9e7e4b0658fc20f979e.

3. "Fiscal Year 2017 ICE Enforcement and Removal Operations Report," ICE.gov, https://www.ice.gov/removal-statistics/2017.

4. Yegneh Torbati, "U.S. Deportations Down in 2017 but Immigration Arrests Up," Reuters, December 5, 2017, https://www.reuters.com/article/us-usa-immigration/u-s-deportations-down-in-2017-but-immigration-arrests-up-idUSKBN1DZ2O5.

5. Julia Horowitz, "Trump's Tall Order: Hiring 15,000 ICE and Border Patrol Agents," CNN Money, https://money.cnn.com/2017/03/03/news/economy/hiring-immigration-agents-ice/index.html.

6. "Immigration and Customs Enforcement: Frequently Asked Questions." ICE.gov, https://www.ice.gov.

7. Julia Horowitz, "Trump's Tall Order: Hiring 15,000 ICE and Border Patrol Agents," CNN Money, https://money.cnn.com/2017/03/03/news/economy/hiring-immigration-agents-ice/index.html.

Chapter 3: ICE and Immigration Law

1. Patrick J. Hayes and Sofya Apteka, *The Making of Modern Immigration: An Encyclopedia of People and Ideas, Volume 1* (Santa Barbara, CA: ABC-CLIO, 2012).

2. "Difference Between U.S. Customs and Border Protection (CBP), U.S. Citizenship and Immigration Services (USCIS) and U.S. Immigration and Customs Enforcement (ICE)," CBP.gov, https://help.cbp.gov/app/answers/detail/a_id/1040/~/difference-between-u.s.-customs-and-border-protection-%28cbp%29%2C-u.s.-citizenship.

3. Ibid.

4. Staff, "Businessman in U.S. 39 Years Deported with Little Notice, Family Says," CBS News, January 30, 2017, https://www.cbsnews.com/news/amer-adi-othman-ohio-businessman-deported-with-little-notice-jordan.

5. Carlo Angerer, "Nazi Collaborator Jakiw Palij Is Deported from U.S. to Germany," NBC News, August 21, 2018, https://www.nbcnews.

com/news/world/nazi-collaborator-jakiw-palij-arrested-new-york-de-ported-germany-n902441.

6. Mallory Simon, "This Is the Face of Deportation: A Dad with No Criminal Record, an American Wife and Two Kids," CNN, July 27, 2017, https://www.cnn.com/2017/07/27/politics/connecticut-family-de-portations/index.html.

Chapter 4: Controversial Decisions

1. "Deaths at Adult Detention Centers," American Immigration Lawyers Association, July 26, 2018, https://www.aila.org/infonet/deaths-at-adult-detention-centers.

2. Nina Bernstein, "Officials Hid Truth of Immigrant Deaths in Jail," *New York Times*, January 9, 2010, https://www.nytimes.com/2010/01/10/us/10detain.html.

3. Leanna Garfield and Shayanne Gal, "Here's How Many ICE Deten-tion Centers Are Holding Immigrants in Every State," *Business Insider*, June 22, 2018, https://www.businessinsider.com/ice-immigrant-fami-lies-dhs-detention-centers-2018-6.

4. "US: Poor Medical Care, Deaths, in Immigrant Detention," Human Rights Watch, https://www.hrw.org/news/2018/06/20/us-poor-medi-cal-care-deaths-immigrant-detention.

5. Mythili Sampathkumar, "Trump Signs Order Overturning Family Separa-tion Policy in Dramatic U-turn After Widespread Anger," *Independent,* June 20, 2018, https://www.independent.co.uk/news/world/americas/us-politics/donald-trump-family-separation-tent-cities-us-mexico-bor-der-immigration-a8408556.html.

6. Julie Watson and Morgan Lee, "Immigrant Families Struggling with Trauma of Separation," Associated Press, September 7, 2018, https://apnews.com/cf1c03a8e9ae4969aa8e331862d6897b.

Chapter 5: The Future of ICE

1. Elaine Godfrey, "What 'Abolish ICE' Actually Means," *Atlantic*, July 11, 2018, https://www.theatlantic.com/politics/archive/2018/07/what-abolish-ice-actually-means/564752.
2. Jaden Urbi, "Here's Who's Making Money from Immigration Enforcement," CNBC, June 29, 2018, https://www.cnbc.com/2018/06/28/companies-profiting-immigration-enforcement-private-sector-prison-tech.html.
3. Julia Glum, "15 Organizations Doing Business with ICE—and How Much They're Making," *Money*, June 27, 2018, http://time.com/money/5318933/organizations-doing-business-with-ice.
4. ICE Agents, "Letter to DHS Secretary Kirstjen Nielsen," US ICE, June 29, 2018, https://www.documentcloud.org/documents/4562896-FILE-3286.html.
5. Haley Hinkle and Rachel Levinson-Waldman, "The Abolish ICE Movement Explained," *Brennan Center for Justice*, July 30, 2018, https://www.brennancenter.org/blog/abolish-ice-movement-explained.
6. Emmet Livingstone, "What Is Schengen?," *Politico*, November 20, 2015, https://www.politico.eu/article/what-is-schengen-explainer-borders-europe-free-movement.

GLOSSARY

abolishment Ending or doing away with something.

asylum The protection given to those who enter a country for safety reasons. Asylum seekers are often fleeing political or religious persecution or gang violence and fear for their lives in their home country.

civil rights The rights of citizens to freedom and equality.

counterfeit A copy of something that was made for the purpose of deceiving others into thinking it is the real thing.

counterterrorism Political or military activities designed to prevent or thwart terrorism or terrorist activity.

cultural property This could include a number of physical items from buildings, museums, religious institutions, statues, works of art, and libraries. Theft or destruction of them has been done by terrorists in order to finance their activities.

customs The official department that administers and collects the duties, or fees, placed by a government on imported goods; the place at a port, airport, or border area where officials check incoming goods, travelers, or luggage.

cyber crime A criminal act done through the use of computers and/or the internet; more generally called hacking.

deportation The action of returning someone to their home country.

detention center A jail or prison where people are kept forcibly because they may have or did commit a crime.

felony A serious crime often involving violence that usually carries a prison sentence of more than one year.

human trafficking Like modern slavery, it involves trading people for forced labor or exploitation.

illegal immigration Entering a country without legal paperwork with the intention to stay or overstaying the visa issued by a government in violation of laws.

migration When a person or group of people travels to a new country to find a better life, whether that means escaping poverty or violence or seeking employment or housing.

minor A person who is a child in the eyes of the law.

naturalization Allowing someone to obtain citizenship of another country.

FURTHER READING

Books

Armenta, Amada. *Protect, Serve, and Deport: The Rise of Policing as Immigration Enforcement*. Oakland, CA: University of California Press, 2017.

Miller, Todd. *Border Patrol Nation: Dispatches from the Front Lines of Homeland Security*. San Francisco, CA: City Lights Books, 2014.

Noorani, Ali. *There Goes the Neighborhood: How Communities Overcome Prejudice and Meet the Challenge of American Immigration*. Amherst, NY: Prometheus Books, 2017.

Tirman, John. *Dream Chasers: Immigration and the American Backlash*. Cambridge, MA: MIT Press, 2015.

Websites

Migration Policy Institute

migrationpolicy.org

This website provides independent analysis of movement of people across borders around the world.

Rand Corporation

rand.org

The Rand Corporation is a research organization that helps develop solutions to public policy issues like immigration law enforcement.

Urban Institute

urban.org

The Urban Institute is a nonprofit research organization collaborating with community activists, government leaders, and businesses to find solutions to policy challenges for immigrant populations.

INDEX